STONE AGE TABLET

3rd January, 100 BC

SPECIAL EDITION

**HAPPY BIRTHDAY
Stone Age Tablet
500,000 years old
TODAY!**

Andrew Langley

raintree

Raintree is an imprint of Capstone Global Library Limited, a company incorporated in England and Wales having its registered office at 264 Banbury Road, Oxford, OX2 7DY – Registered company number: 6695582

www.raintree.co.uk
myorders@raintree.co.uk

Edited by Penny West and Helen Cox Cannons
Designed by Philippa Jenkins
Illustrated by Philippa Jenkins
Picture research by Kelly Garvin
Originated by Capstone Global Library Ltd
Produced by Victoria Fitzgerald
Printed and bound in China

ISBN 978 1 4747 1654 3
19 18 17 16 15
10 9 8 7 6 5 4 3 2 1

ISBN 978 1 4747 1655 0
21 20 19 18 17
10 9 8 7 6 5 4 3 2 1

British Library Cataloguing in Publication Data
A full catalogue record for this book is available from the British Library.

Acknowledgements
We would like to thank the following for permission to reproduce photographs: Alamy: Chris Howes/Wild Places Photography, 10, Countryside Collection/Homer Sykes, 7, Doug Houghton, 28 (top), George Sweeney, 26, Ian Franics, 27, MS Bretherton, 20, Powered by Light/Alan Spencer, 25 (middle); Bridgeman Images/Judith Dobie, 21; Charles Tait Photographic, 9; Dreamstime: duming, 16, Ian Keirle, 23 (right); Framepool, 13; Getty Images: Andrew Holt, 23 (left), De Agostini Picture Library, 5 (top right); Newscom: World History Archive, 18 (bottom); Photo by Justin Hoffman, 19 (b); Philippa Jenkins, 15; Prehistoric Man as depicted by Will Lord, image courtesy of The Higgins Art Gallery and Museum, Bedford/www.Will-Loed.co.uk, 11; Shutterstock: Africa Studio, 25, bonga1965, 25, Brent Hofacker, 25, CREATISTA, 17, Danita Delmont, cover (bottom right), Dja65, cover (tr), Dr.G, 25, duchy, 22 (l), Elnur, 24, Eric Isselee, 5 (br), GG Pro Photo, 18 (t), Incredible Arctic, 12, iurii, 14, Jaroslava V 8, Jason Benz Bennee, 28 (b), Jean-Philippe Menard, 4 (top left), Josef Hanus, 19 (t), Kachalkina Veronika, cover (bottom left)(br), 25, Orhan Cam, 25, Platslee, 6, Shots Studio, 25, Sophie Louise Davis, 18 (t), Stewart Smith Photography, cover (t), QArts, 25, Yarygin, 4 (bl), Zemler, 16; The Image Works/English Heritage/Mary Evans, 22 (r); Wikimedia: Geni/GFDL CC-BY-SA, 18, John O'Neill, cover (bl)

Artistic Elements: Shutterstock; David M. Schrader, J. Schelkle

We would like to thank Dr Oliver Harris at the University of Leicester for his invaluable help in the preparation of this book.

Some words are shown in bold, **like this**. You can find out what they mean by looking in the glossary.

INSIDE...

SPECIAL EDITION

Note from the editor:

Welcome to a special edition of the *Stone Age Tablet*. This year the *Tablet* is an amazing 500,000 years old!

It goes all the way back to the Stone Age, when the very first British people made tools and weapons out of stone. Next came the **Bronze** Age, when we used metal for the first time. After that, of course, is the period we live in today – the Iron Age.

To celebrate, we've put together a selection of our all-time greatest news stories across the ages, organized by subject. You will find the dates beside each article. We hope you enjoy this look back at the past – and the present!

DESIRABLE PROPERTIES FOR SALE
see page 22

14th April, 490 BC

iron spear

sharper stronger harder cheaper

iron axe heads

What's so great about iron?

Everyone's talking about iron. It's today's must-have material. But is it all it's cracked up to be? We asked master blacksmith Sled Jammer to give us five reasons to love the new metal:

- Iron swords are much sharper than bronze ones
- Iron is harder than stone and bronze
- It's much easier to find than copper or tin (which make bronze)
- It's cheaper

2nd October, 500,000 BC

LION AGE

Life's pretty dangerous in Sussex. The people of Boxgrove share their land with big game. Bears, rhinos, giant deer and even lions have all been seen there.

Essex, 6400 BC

BRITAIN CUT OFF!

Rising seas break land link with Europe

It's official – we live on islands. For centuries, the sea has been rising. Now it has washed over the last piece of dry land linking us to Europe.

So Great Britain and Ireland are surrounded by water. This means people can't walk to the continent any longer. We'll have to go by boat.

Has the sea risen because of climate change? Yes, says weather expert Hayley Snow:

"The air has slowly been getting hotter, and has melted a lot of the ice in the north. The water has run into the sea, making it deeper and covering lower areas of land."

Norfolk, 2049 BC

HENGE BY THE SEA

Britain's newest **henge**, or timber circle, stands proudly on a beach. Over 200 people came here to Norfolk to build what they call Seahenge. They dug a huge hole and planted a full-grown oak tree in it – upside down.

Why? One worker told us they hoped it would grow downwards into the earth. The builders believe there is another world under the ground, where spirits live.

Wiltshire, 2400 BC

Record Breaker

SILBURY HILL is the highest human-made mound in all of Europe. Officials reckon it is 30 metres (98 feet) high – the height of 16 men. This makes it as big as the pyramids now being built in Egypt as we write.

RELIGIOUS NEWS

CLASH OVER HOLY SITE

Plans to extend Stonehenge

Britain's biggest stone circle is about to get even bigger. New plans show how far this sacred burial site will grow.

The present blue stones will be surrounded by a new ring of gigantic stones called sarsens. These monsters will stand upright in pairs, and each pair will have a third sarsen resting on top. The work is expected to take a few hundred years to complete.

But not everyone is happy with the idea. "It's stupid" said one local resident. "Going to all this trouble for a circle of old stones? I can't see many people coming to look at that!"

It's stupid

North Wales, 100 BC

Mistletoe Men

Our Welsh **correspondent** reports on a big religious festival

The annual **mistletoe** cutting took place here today. Special priests called **druids** put on white robes for the ceremony. Some climbed into an oak tree, and cut off branches of mistletoe with golden sickles. The mistletoe was brewed into a sacred drink, which will make sure there is a bumper harvest this year.

Orkney, 22nd December, 2800 BC

MIDWINTER MAGIC

Yesterday was the shortest day of the year. Hundreds of people came to the great tomb at Maeshowe at sunset yesterday. They watched as the last of the sunlight shone down the tomb's passageway.

North Wales, 1500 BC

KINGS OF COPPER

Our Metal correspondent, Tina Miner, visits Britain's biggest mine

Ever wondered where bronze comes from? You'll find part of the answer here at the monster copper mine at Great Orme in North Wales.

It's a long way down into the mine. The main shaft is over 70 metres (230 feet) deep. That's the height of 40 people. To get to the bottom you have to use flimsy ladders made of rope and timber! Out of this vast hole comes load after load of copper. It is hacked from the earth by miners, who use hammers made of stone and bone. The copper is melted and mixed with tin to make – bronze!

100 BC

Money News

LOOK OUT FOR A NEW KIND OF MONEY: iron bars as long as your arm. They are being used in southern Britain to buy goods. But some people complain the bars are too big and heavy to carry about (see letters to the editor, page 15).

Suffolk, 400,000 BC

CAUGHT KNAPPING!

The *Tablet* talks to Hugh Jax, Britain's best flint worker

"I 'm a knapper. I take a lump of flint and "knap" it – that means hitting it with a stone hammer. If you hit it right, a flake breaks off. Then another, then another. I shape the flint into a hand axe. One end has a blade. The other end is rounded. You hold it in your hand and use it to chop wood or cut meat. But take care – it's very sharp!"

DOWN ON THE FARM: HERD THE LATEST?

Following the reindeer

In the hills of Derbyshire, a group of hunters looks for reindeer. "There they are," says the leader. He points to a long line of reindeer on a ridge. "We follow them all summer."

The herd is vital to this group of hunters. They eat reindeer meat, and wear clothes of reindeer skin. But the herd doesn't stay still. It moves hundreds of miles every year, searching for food. So the hunters keep close, killing an animal whenever they need to. As well as reindeer, they hunt horses, red deer and wild pigs.

These hunters are among the many bands that trek across Europe and into Britain. They have no settled homes.

Somerset, 190 BC

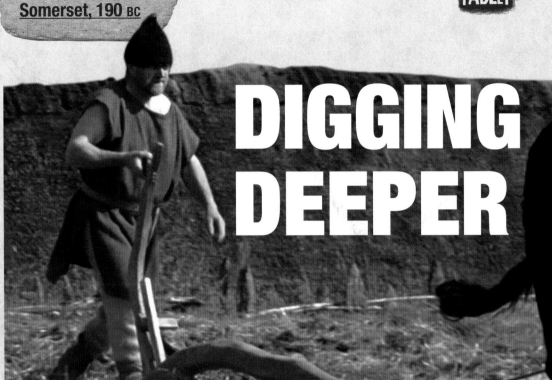

DIGGING DEEPER

New iron plough hits the West

Growing your own crops just got easier. For centuries, farmers have struggled with wooden ploughs. They barely scratched the surface of the soil, and were always getting broken.

Now, thanks to the Iron Age, they've got a new kind of plough. Called an **ard**, it has an iron tip. Pulled along by two oxen, the ard rips much deeper into the earth than older wooden ploughs. It is so tough that farmers can dig up heavy land full of clay and stones.

Somerset farmer Bill Hook loves his new plough. It helps him to grow much more wheat and other crops.

"Now we never go hungry in winter,"

he boasts.

Cumbria, 3700 BC

A DAY IN THE LIFE
This week....

THE AXE FACTORY IN THE SKY

Fancy working on top of a mountain? Jim Laker does it every day. He climbs up Pike of Stickle, a high and lonely mountain in Langdale. "The views are amazing," he says, "but it's a bit scary."

Jim works in an axe factory. It's in the open air, on the edge of a steep drop to the valley below. Why is it here?

> "Because of the rock, called greenstone. It's perfect for making axe heads."

First, Jim builds a fire to crack off pieces of rock. Then he chips and hammers to shape a sharp axe head. Finally he polishes the green rock smooth. "Beautiful, isn't it?" he says. Langdale axes are now being used all over Britain and Ireland.

Letters to the editor...

the page where you tell Britain what you think

Save our forests

Why are we cutting down so many trees? If we carry on like this, our wild woods will vanish. Let's preserve them now!

Yours sincerely

IRMA GREENIE

York, 2000 BC

Hurray for immigrants!

Some people grumble about the bands of foreigners coming to Britain from Europe. This is stupid. **Immigrants** bring lots of new skills, and work hard to create new farmland and build new villages. We should make them welcome.

Yours sincerely

ARCHIE TECT

North Wales, 3800 BC

Money too heavy?

I always like to carry some money around with me. But modern cash is just too big. Yesterday I dropped one of the new iron coins on my toe. Now I have a giant bruise. I think the government should do something about this.

Yours sincerely

DORIS MCBUNION

Scotland, 100 BC

"What have I told you about drawing on the walls?"

Gower Peninsula, 30,000 BC

CELEB NEWS
First with the latest about people who matter

THE "RED LADY" IS REALLY A MAN

Now we know. The "Red Lady of Paviland" in her scarlet dress became the most talked-about person in South Wales. "She" wore lots of red makeup, as well as jewellery made from sea shells. But today we can reveal the amazing truth behind the legend. She is actually a he! A 21 year-old local man has admitted dressing up as the "Red Lady". He told the *Tablet* "I did it for a dare, and it seemed to catch on!"

Wiltshire, 2300 BC

AMESBURY ARCHER

Who is the mystery man behind the new bid to develop Stonehenge? The *Tablet* has learned that he is none other than Amesbury Archer. The 35 year-old local chieftain was born in Switzerland, but has built up his wealth in Britain. He is pushing for a vast new ring of stones to be erected in Wiltshire (see page 8).

Clonycavan, 300 BC

BAD NEWS FOR GINGER

The IRISH KING is not popular. This year's harvest has been terrible, and many people are going hungry. The king gets the blame for this. And if things don't improve, he could be put to death. Many people already laugh at the king because of his elaborate hairdo. He keeps his hair in place with a special gel made of oil and pine resin.

FASHION HIGHLIGHTS

Yorkshire, 7500 BC

DEER ME!

If you want to catch a deer, you've got to look like one. This stylish helmet is made from a red deer skull – complete with antlers. Easy-to-use straps keep it firmly on your head. Dressed in the antler hat, every hunter can get close to his prey without being spotted.

Southern Scotland, 2000 BC

JET SET

Everybody wants jet. This shiny black stone is very rare in Britain, but it can be made into the most beautiful jewellery. The latest treasure is a jet necklace, made of 130 pieces!

North Wales, 1700 BC

Mold Gold

Here's the perfect present for a great warrior – the Mold Cape. It is made from a single piece of gold, beaten into a thin sheet and brilliantly decorated. The cape sits snugly on the shoulders, and it is lined with the finest leather to keep you warm.

HANDY HINTS

OLD SETH ANSWERS YOUR QUERIES

Prehistoric Press, 6,500 BC

Q: We've killed a huge elk and eaten most of the meat. What can we do with the rest of it? There's loads!

A: Don't throw anything away. Use the antlers as spades. Clean and dry the skin to make clothes. The bones make good tools, and the **sinews** can be twisted into ropes. For more details, see my book *101 Uses for a Dead Elk.*

Q. I'm freezing! How do I light a fire?

A: You need a stick with a pointed end, and a piece of wood with a small hole in the middle. Put the stick into the hole and rub it between your palms so that it spins back and forth. Keep going until it gets hot. Put sawdust on it and keep on spinning. In the end, you'll make a fire. Good luck!

Q. I want to paint a cave wall, but DIY shops haven't been invented yet. How do I make different coloured paints?

A: It all depends where you live. If you're lucky, you can find **ochre** (a mixture of clay and rock) in the ground. This gives you yellow, red and orange colours. For black, use burned bones or charcoal. For white, use a white clay called kaolin. Grind each of these into a powder, using a big stone. Then mix the powder with water and fat to make a paste. Now get painting!

TRAVEL NEWS

Somerset, 3807 BC

No more wet feet
New track built over marshes

It's very soggy down here on the Somerset Levels. Winter is worst, when many fields are flooded. For years, travellers trying to get across have sunk into the **peaty** mud up to their knees.

But now local farmers are building a new wooden walkway across the marshes. It is known as the Sweet Track. They hope this will encourage more people to visit the area. It seems to be working. Many traders and craftworkers are coming to the Levels to sell their goods.

How are the farmers doing it? First, they laid two lines of poles on top of the peat. Then, they drove in long pegs at an angle to hold the poles in place. Over the top, they fixed planks for walking on. You can walk along without getting wet at all.

Dover, 1500 BC

OVER THE SEA
Dover boat launch

Book your ticket for France today! A new boat launched in Dover is going to make crossing the Channel a lot easier. The Dover Boat is probably the biggest ever built – at over 10 metres (33 feet), it's as long as six people. That means plenty of room for passengers and cargo. It's also wide enough for two people to sit side by side – much more comfortable than those old-fashioned canoes carved out of tree trunks.

Leicester, 200 BC

World speed record broken

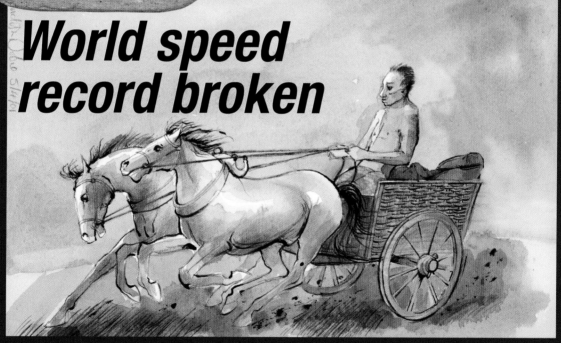

Daredevil Charlie O'Teer became the fastest man in Britain today. In his two-horse chariot, he touched speeds of more than 30 kilometres (20 miles) per hour. He puts his success down to his new iron tyres.

HOMES

Bargain of the week

Skara Brae, ORKNEY

A rare chance to buy a beautiful dwelling that's older than Stonehenge. Built of local stone and thatch, it is set in a natural hollow to give protection from the wild weather. There is plenty of storage space, plus a built-in fireplace and dresser. Modern features include a water storage tank and a sewer. Hurry! This is sure to be snapped up fast.

Price: 10 cows and 36 sheep

Maiden Castle, DORSET

Here's a safe place to raise your kids. This timber and thatch house is set inside the biggest hill fort in Britain. It is surrounded by two high earth banks, with a deep ditch between them. And it's on top of a hill. No unwanted raiders here!

*Price: 8 gold **ingots***

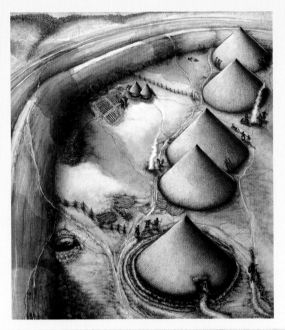

FOR SALE

Cheddar, SOMERSET

A cave of your very own in lovely Cheddar Gorge! There's plenty of space in here to suit a big family. Features include solid stone walls, **stalactites** in every room and a colony of horseshoe bats. There's easy access to fresh water in the river outside.
Price: 98 red deer antlers

Castle Henllys, PEMBROKESHIRE

Nice and snug: this eco-friendly roundhouse is built with the latest Iron Age technology. The curved walls are made of hazel branches, covered with clay, straw and animal dung. This method keeps the cold out and the heat in. A drainage ditch is dug round the house to prevent flooding.
Price: 10 iron bars

Enniskillen, FERMANAGH

Fancy living on water? Then snap up this **crannog**, set prettily on a Northern Irish lake. Built on sturdy stilts, the timber house is just the right size for a small family. You'll never run short of water – or fish!
Price: 20 rolls of woollen cloth

Food and Drink

Is the iron-age diet good for you?

The *Tablet's* food correspondent, Ivor Bigtum, looks at the evidence.

Are we eating the right things these days? Most people eat lots of **starchy** food – barley porridge, wheat bread and stews. The lucky ones have cheese as well. But is this a healthy diet? These foods may be making us too fat. And all that sugary honey could be ruining our teeth.

Maybe we should be more like our Stone Age ancestors. They were healthier and fitter back in **Palaeolithic** times. Of course, these hunters lived very active lives. Running after deer uses up a large amount of energy.

So what was the Palaeo Diet? Here's what people ate half a million years ago:

- Fresh meat (anything from bears and reindeer to birds and wild pigs)

- Eggs

- Seafood, including fish, crab, mussels, oysters and lobster

- Plant food, such as wild berries, nuts, herbs, leaves, vegetables.

That's about it. It's all very fresh and healthy. But don't you think it would have got a bit boring, day after day? Maybe wheat bread and stew don't sound so bad after all!

2500 BC

Stale into ale!

<u>A great way to use up old bread</u>

Beer is very popular over in Europe. So here's an easy recipe for making it, using stale bread.

- Break the bread into pieces, and then soak it in water. It should start frothing after a day or two.
- Drain off the liquid — that's the beer.
- Scrape off the froth and use it as **yeast** for making more bread.
- Throw the old bread to the pigs. Everybody's happy!

ARTS AND

Guide to the best music gigs

Kerry bronze trumpets blare

Rock 'n' Bone
Sussex: 2800 BC

Together again for one night only – the greatest Stone Age band! It features the classic Rock 'n' Bone sound, unchanged since the Ice Age. Up front are the sweet sounds of flutes made of bird bones and stones, together with the honk of animal horns. And behind them is the rhythm section, the clang of rocks and the clack of cow bones.

Heavy metal night
Kerry, Ireland: 900 BC

Come and hear the blare of the bronze horns and the roar of the curved trumpet (left). It will be loud! If that's not enough, get deafened by the metal bells called **crotals**. For something quieter, there are the lovely wooden pipes of Wicklow.

Battlecry
Banffshire, Scotland: 100 BC

Want to hear a **carnyx**? It's all the rage. At one time this mighty horn was blown to send our soldiers into battle and frighten the enemy. But now the carnyx is thrilling audiences all over Scotland. It's as tall as a man, and makes a terrifying sound. No wonder our enemies ran away!

ENTERTAINMENT

Creswell Crags, Derbyshire, 11,000 BC

Art Review

Arts correspondent, Birdie Honour-Wall

Birds, bears and bison

Hurry along to Creswell Crags for an amazing exhibition of cave art. Artists have been hard at work for weeks in Church Hole, one of the caves here.

They have used the natural shapes in the rock, carving them to show all sorts of animals. There are bison, bears, horses and deer. Best of all is a figure of a bird with a long curved bill.

FOR SALE

HOUSEHOLD

Bronze mirror
Highly polished so you can see exactly what you look like.

Large clay pot
Can be hung over a cooking fire. Ideal for making stews and casseroles.

Pot of red ochre make-up
As worn by the Red Lady of Paviland.

Beautiful jet necklace
Very rare antique item, made in Yorkshire.

Granite quern for sale (below)
Top quality **quern**! Unwanted Beltane present.

FARM AND GARDEN

Pair of wooden wheels
Nearly new. Could be used for farm cart or old-fashioned chariot.

Bronze axe
Good for chopping wood or fighting in battles. One careful owner.

Garden spade
Made of pure reindeer antler – the best or your money back!

Large pile of flint
Ideal for knapping into blades for knives, arrowheads or axes. Owner retiring from flint business after more than 40 years. Buyer collects – will need own cart.

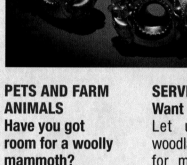

PETS AND FARM ANIMALS

Have you got room for a woolly mammoth?
This one-year-old needs a lot of space but could make a perfect pet for your kids. Healthy and house-trained.

Six sheep
Produce lots of wool for weaving cloth. Can also be used to mow the lawn.

Big dog
Good for guarding the house. He'll bark at everybody – whether you want him to or not!

Baby rhinoceros
It has grown too big for our house. Free to good home.

SERVICES

Want a bigger farm?
Let us clear your woodland, giving space for more fields and more crops. Contact Axeman Tree Care for a quote.

Henges 'R' Us Ltd
We build everything from stone circles to hill forts. No job too small.

Room in the Tomb!
Bury your loved ones at Carrowmore, Ireland. This smart new grave complex has plenty of space for all the family.

Torc of the town.
Torc neck rings (above) made to order, hand crafted from bronze, copper, iron or even gold. Get our free catalogue.

TIMELINE

The Stone Age

500,000 BC
First humans arrive in Britain; makers of flint hand axes live in Boxgrove, Sussex; bands of hunter-gatherers roam the land (until about 5000 BC)

30,000 BC
"Red Lady" of Paviland buried in South Wales

11,000 BC
Cave paintings and sculptures created at Creswell Crags, Derbyshire

10,000 BC
Last Ice Age ends: climate gets warmer

6500 BC
Britain and Ireland become separate islands as seas rise

4000 BC
The start of farming

3600 BC
Axe making begins at Langdale in Cumbria

3900 BC
Sweet Track built in Somerset

3000 BC
Maeshowe chambered tomb built in Orkney

2500 BC
Main stone circle built at Stonehenge

2400 BC
Silbury Hill constructed in Wiltshire

The Bronze Age

2150 BC
Britons learn to make bronze

2049 BC
Seahenge built in Norfolk

2000 BC
Copper mine started at Great Orme in North Wales

1700 BC
The Mold Cape is made of beaten gold in North Wales

1500 BC
Dover boat launched

The Iron Age

750 BC
Britons learn to make tools and weapons out of iron

300 BC
Clonycavan Man buried in Meath, Ireland

190 BC
Iron-tipped ploughs called ards are used in Britain

100 BC
Special iron bars are used as money

Glossary

ard simple Iron Age wooden plough with an iron point, which scratches the soil deeply

bronze metal made by mixing copper and tin

carnyx long, bronze, trumpet-like musical instrument with a bell shape at the end. It was used in the Bronze Age and Iron Age.

correspondent special reporter writing for the *Stone Age Tablet*

crannog ancient house made of timber and built in a lake or marsh in Scotland or Ireland. They were built on stilts to keep dry.

crotal bronze bell with a metal ball inside, which rang when it was shaken

druid priest in Iron Age Britain. This was long before Christianity or any other organized religion came to Britain. Druids probably worshipped many nature spirits.

henge earthen enclosure where a bank is outside a ditch, often with a circle of stone or timber posts. These were probably built for religious ceremonies.

immigrant person who moves out of one country to live in another. During the long Ice Age, nobody lived in Britain at all – it was too cold. So everyone who became British later was originally an immigrant!

ingot piece of metal ready to be melted and cast or hammered into a new shape

mistletoe plant with white berries that grows on trees

ochre mixture of earth and clay that is found in the ground: it can be red, yellow or brown and is used for colouring other things

Palaeolithic early part of the Stone Age, when the first stone tools were made

peat black mud made from decayed and squashed plants

quern simple tool for grinding wheat and other grains into flour: it is made of two stone wheels, one on top of the other

sinew bunch of tough fibres that connect our muscles to our bones. Stone Age hunters used the sinews from animals they killed to made threads and cords.

stalactite rocky spike hanging from the roof of a cave: it is made by dripping water, which leaves traces of stone behind

starch substance made mostly of sugars. Starch is found in wheat and other grains, as well as potatoes.

torc metal ring made to wear round the neck. Many beautiful torcs were made of bronze or gold.

yeast tiny fungus that is mixed with grain to make bread or beer

Find out more

Books

Changes in Britain from the Stone Age to the Iron Age, Claire Throp (Raintree, 2015)

Life in the Stone Age, Bronze Age and Iron Age, Anita Ganeri (Raintree, 2014)

Prehistory, Hands on: A Creative Journey into Ancient Britain, Catherine Henderson (Celtic Harmony, 2014)

Stone Age Bone Age!: A Book About Prehistoric People, Mick Manning and Brita Granstrom (Franklin Watts, 2014)

Websites

www.bbc.co.uk/history/handsonhistory/ancient-britain.shtml
Videos, facts and projects can be found on this BBC website.

primaryhomeworkhelp.co.uk/timeline.html
This website includes a useful timeline of prehistoric Britain.

Places to visit in Britain

Here are just a few of the many great prehistoric sites you can visit. Is there one near you?

Cheddar Gorge
Somerset BS27 3QF
Huge caves and a museum of local finds

Creswell Crags
Worksop, Nottinghamshire S80 3LH
Caves, cave art and a wonderful Ice Age exhibition

Dover Museum
Dover, Kent CT16 1PB
The amazing Dover boat from the Bronze Age

Great Orme Mines
Llandudno, Wales LL30 2XG
The underground mines where copper was dug out long ago

Skara Brae
Sandwick, Orkney KW16 3LR
Stone Age settlement by the sea

Stonehenge
Amesbury, Wiltshire SP4 7DE
The most famous ancient site in Britain

Index